BIBLE
CROSSWORDS
for Kids

D0650513

BARBOUR
PUBLISHING, INC.
Uhrichsville, Ohio

© MCMXCVIII by Barbour Publishing, Inc.

ISBN 1-57748-184-4

Published by Barbour Publishing, Inc.
     P.O. Box 719
     Uhrichsville, OH 44683
     http://www.barbourbooks.com

 Member of the
Evangelical Christian
Publishers Association

Printed in the United States of America.

BIBLE
CROSSWORDS
for Kids

#1

ACROSS

1. Made a joyful noise
5. Belonging to an Egyptian ruler
9. Spanish for the U.S. (Estados Unidos, abbr.)
10. Mountain, abbr.
11. Ohio, abbr.
12. Something that makes music louder, for short
14. Another spelling of the girl's name May
15. To exist
16. Emergency room, abbr.
17. Illinois, abbr.
18. Los Angeles, for short
20. Do, re, me, fa, _____
22. "_____ now thy Creator in the days of thy youth" (Eccles. 12:1)
25. Toy that goes up and down on a string

DOWN

1. South America, abbr.
2. "_____ yourselves likewise with the same mind" (1 Pet. 4:1)
3. Nathan, for short
4. "___ ye therefore" (Matt. 28:19)
5. Vegetable that grows in a pod
6. "_____ yourselves therefore under

	1	2	3	4		
5	6				7	8
9			10		11	
12		13		14		
	15			16		
17			18	19	20	21
22		23		24		
		25				

the mighty hand of God" (1 Pet. 5:6)

7. What you are when your throat is sore and scratchy
8. Not a he but a _____
13. Class that makes you sweaty, abbr.

14. Myself
17. Infrared, abbr.
18. Name for a lion
19. Girl's name
21. Operating room, abbr.
23. Belonging to me
24. Little _____ Peep

#2 PUZZLE

ACROSS

1. Bomb, slang
5. The foster father of Jesus
7. "More to be desired are they than gold. . .sweeter also than _____ and the honeycomb" (Ps. 19:10)
8. Land where Abram was born (Gen. 11:31)
10. A card game, means "one" in Spanish
11. Many years _____
12. City in Nevada, _____ Vegas
13. Small bed
14. What the doctor wants you to say when you open your mouth
15. Scripture section
17. Bottom of foot
18. Night birds

DOWN

1. Things you're not supposed to do
2. "_____ hospitality one to another without grudging" (1 Pet. 4:9)
3. "I saw a star fall from heaven. . . and to him was given the _____ of the bottomless pit" (Rev. 9:1)
4. Extended play, abbr.

5. This man was swallowed by a great fish
6. Belonging to Hugo
7. A kind of hoop
9. A way to learn
11. Pieces of land
15. Promise
16. Wing of a building
17. ___ what?

#3 PUZZLE

ACROSS

1. Person who speaks Arabic
5. "Hearken unto me, my people; and give _____ unto me" (Isa. 51:4)
8. Infant
9. Pimple, slang
10. People who swing
12. All right
13. The king of the Amalekites that Samuel cut into pieces (1 Sam. 15:33)
16. Three, in Roman numerals
19. Things that drip
21. To be sick
22. Esau's father-in-law (2 Gen. 26:34)
23. Mountain, abbr.
24. "I beheld, and, lo, there _____ _____ no man, and all the birds of the heavens were fled" (2 words) (Jer. 4:25)

DOWN

1. Stomach muscles, for short
2. Not cooked
3. One of King David's wives (1 Sam. 25:39)
4. Benjamin, for short
5. Belonging to one of the prophets
6. What we breathe

1	**2**	**3**	**4**	■	**5**	**6**	**7**
8				■	**9**		
10			**11**				
■				**12**		■	■
13	**14**		**15**		**16**	**17**	**18**
19				**20**			
21			■	**22**			
23		■	**24**				

7. Routes, abbr.
11. "_____ ye into all the world, and preach the gospel" (Mark 16:15)
13. The first man
14. What some people do to their teeth while they're sleeping
15. General practitioner, abbr.
17. Metal
18. "There _____ _____ God like thee in the heaven" (2 words) (2 Chron. 6:14)
20. A green vegetable

#4

ACROSS

1. Flying mammal
4. Beatrice, for short
7. A person from the church at Ephesus
10. Animals with antlers
11. Route, abbr.
12. Railroad, abbr.
13. Good _____ gold
14. Nebraska, abbr.
15. "_____ the world hate you, ye know that it hated me before" (John 15:18)
16. Gym class, abbr.
17. "_____ thou into the joy of thy lord" (Matt. 25:21)
20. One of the three men thrown into the fiery furnace (Dan. 3:20)
22. Neither
23. Steal

DOWN

1. Where you sleep at night
2. Big monkey
3. "_____ is therefore now no condemnation to those who are in Christ Jesus" (Rom. 8:1)
4. Prefix that means "two"
5. What you hear with
6. "Go to the _____, thou sluggard" (Prov. 6:6)

8. To make a mistake
9. Sunday school, abbr.
13. The opposite of before
14. The mountain where Moses died (Deut. 34:1, 5)
15. Place where Mary and Joseph could find no room
16. Something you cook in
17. Edward, for short
18. Your sense of yourself
19. Robert, for short
21. Emergency room, abbr.

#5 PUZZLE

ACROSS

2. A city attacked by King Asa's troops (1 Kings 15:20)
7. "_____ one another" (Rom. 15:14)
10. Bottom of a skirt
11. Another spelling of Noah (Matt. 24:37)
12. ___ what?
13. To make clothes
14. Infrared, abbr.
15. Swallowed food
16. Paintings, statues, etc.
17. Establishment, abbr.
19. "Thy faithfulness _____ unto the clouds" (Ps. 36:5)
22. Borrowed money

DOWN

1. A name for God (Ps. 68:4)
2. Something that never dies
3. Short for Josephine
4. The opposite of off
5. Roman numeral XIX
6. Not a he
8. "As newborn babes, _____ the sincere milk of the word" (1 Pet. 2:2)
9. "that which thou _____ is not quickened, except it die" (1 Cor. 15:36)

1		2	3	4	5		6
7	8					9	
10					11		
	12			13			
	14			15			
16					17		18
19			20	21			
		22					

13. South America, abbr.
16. ____ you ready?
18. ____ end
20. Company, abbr.
21. The sound of laughter

#6 PUZZLE

ACROSS

1. What a car is that's not new
5. Like ice
7. A laugh
8. Abraham's birthplace (Gen. 11:31)
9. Pretty ___ a picture
11. God's name for Himself, I ____ (Ex. 3:14)
12. Note in the musical scale
13. Not a she but a ____
14. Get __ of that
16. Small rug
17. The land where Jeremiah lived (Jer. 1:1)
20. "He that refuseth reproof ____" (Prov. 10:17)
21. City in Syria where Paul traveled to (Acts 21:3)

DOWN

1. Chaldean city (Neh. 9:7)
2. The eternal part of a person
3. Book of the Old Testament
4. Delaware, abbr.
5. "That food shall be for store to the land against the seven years of ___" (Gen. 41:36)

6. One of the sons of Reuel (Gen. 36:13)
7. Land where God brought the Reubenites, near the river Gozan (1 Chron. 5:26)
10. Third son of Adam (Gen. 5:3)
15. ___ board
16. "Let me pull out the ___ out of thine eye" (Matt. 7:4)
18. Attempt
19. Not him

ACROSS

1. Company, abbr.
3. Habakkuk, abbr.
6. Pharaoh's wife, the queen (1 Kings 11:19)
9. Not she but ____
10. God created us in His own ____
11. Rises in the east
13. Form of no
14. My sock ____ holes
15. Hole in the ground
16. Hittite man (1 Kings 15:5)
18. Note on the musical scale
20. People who aren't Jews
22. How old you are
23. Opposite of off

DOWN

1. Where Peter went to live to escape Herod (Acts 12:19)
2. Ohio, abbr.
3. Bottom of a skirt
4. A son of Elio-enai, a descendent of David (1 Chron. 3:24)
5. "For God so loved the world that he gave his only ____ Son" (John 3:16)
6. Thursday, abbr.

7. Sharp fastener
8. ___ the table
12. Making use of
14. Squeeze someone with your arms
15. 21st letter of the Greek alphabet
17. Took in food
19. Isaiah, abbr.
21. "____, I am with you alway" (Matt. 28:20)

#8

ACROSS

1. Things the disciples used to catch fish
5. People who lived in the mountains (Num. 13:29)
9. South America, abbr.
10. Son of Elio-enai, descendent of David (1 Chron. 3:24)
11. "_____ profane and vain babblings " (2 Tim. 2:16)
13. Irish Republican Army, abbr.
14. _____ apple
15. The opposite of yes
16. A chief of Zebulun, (Num. 1:9)
19. Move
21. Filled up and satisfied
23. "Arise, take up _____ bed, and go" (Matt. 9:6)
24. Not new

DOWN

1. Not yes
2. One of the children of Israel, forefather of the Eranites (Num. 26:36)
3. Type of metal
4. A soiled spot on clothing
5. Animal that Jesus rode on Palm Sunday
6. Son of Hammoleketh (1 Chron. 7:18)

7. Where Jonathan and Ahimaaz stayed to hide from Absalom (2 Sam. 17:17)

8. "The children of _____," (Neh. 7:47)

12. "Dwell together in ___" (Ps. 133:1)

16. Establishment, abbr.

17. Gibeon was greater than this city (Josh. 10:2)

18. Bachelor of Arts, abbr.

20. Strange

22. "For God sent not his Son. . ._____ condemn the world" (John 3:17)

#9 PUZZLE

ACROSS

1. Big monkeys
5. "Let us run with _____ the race set before us" (Heb. 12:1)
9. Not off but ___
10. Some people thought Jesus was the reincarnation of this man (Matt. 16:14)
11. Short sleep times
13. Public Broadcasting Service, abbr.
14. Stop living
15. Continent where Jesus lived
16. Our enemy
18. New York, abbr.
19. "The whole _____ _____ sick, and the whole heart faint" (2 words) (Isa. 1:5)
21. Streams of light

DOWN

1. No one's _____ home
2. Desserts
3. Long, narrow fish
4. Uses scissors
5. Small lakes
6. "Shema, and ___" (Neh. 8:4)
7. Cottages
8. A nonfiction short writing

12. The disciple who walked on water
15. Boy's name
17. American Automobile Association, abbr.
20. "Greater ____ he that is in you" (I John 4:4)

#10

ACROSS
1. "Unto ___" (Josh. 13:4)
6. "Be ye doers of the word, and not ___ only" (James 1:22)
9. Blows wind to cool
10. Pay what is ___
11. Either
12. Alike
13. The son of Abdiel (1 Chron. 5:15)
15. Forefather of the Arodites (Num. 26:17)
16. Leviticus, abbr.
17. United States, abbr.
18. False report against someone
22. Parts of jackets that keep heads warm

DOWN
1. "Families of ___" (1 Chron. 4:8)
2. Ink writing instrument
3. Laughter sound
4. Emergency room, abbr.
5. A son of Ishmael (Gen. 25:13)
7. "Ye shall hear of wars and ___ of wars" (Matt. 24:6)
8. Things to plant in the ground

9. Baby horses
12. South America, abbr.
14. "Where are the gods of. . .____?"
(2 Kings 18:34)
19. Opposite of yes
20. Perform

21. Short for Edwin

#11

ACROSS

1. One of Job's friends, Bildad the ____ (Job 2:11)
8. Two Old Testament prophets, ____ and ____
9. New Mexico, abbr.
10. Utah, abbr.
11. Woman's name
13. Right hand, abbr.
14. "____ my people. . .shall humble themselves" (2 Chron. 7:14)
15. Full of understanding
16. Trademark, abbr.
17. Open up and say ____
18. "The women wove ____ for the grove" (2 Kings 23:7)
22. What a person does when her nose tickles

DOWN

1. Note on the musical scale
2. Not she
3. A bone in your arm
4. One of Noah's sons (Gen. 5:32)
5. Contraction for "I am"
6. Sightseeing trips
7. Belonging to the Jewess who became the queen of Persia

8. Belonging to the first wife of Esau (Gen. 26:34)
12. One of the names for Christ: the Son ____ ____ (2 words)
15. Buzz
17. The years you've lived
19. Nebraska, abbr.
20. A compass point, abbr.
21. Girl Scouts, abbr.

#12

ACROSS

1. "He scattereth the ____-frost" (Ps. 147:16)
5. The opposite of lower
7. Set down
8. Neither
10. Establishment, abbr.
11. Not busy
12. One of Benjamin's sons (Gen. 46:21)
13. "Send ye the lamb to the ruler of the land from ____ to the wilderness" (Isa. 16:1)
14. "Let us slay him, and cast him into some ___" (Gen. 37:20)
15. _____, white, and blue
16. "The body is not one ____ but many" (1 Cor. 12:14)
19. What you plant

DOWN

1. "Israel dwelt among the ____" (Judg. 3:5)
2. One of the peoples destroyed by the Israelites (Josh. 2:10)
3. What you say when the doctor looks at your throat
4. "The recompence of a man's hands shall be ____ unto him" (Prov. 12:14)

5. Son of Dan
   (Gen. 46:23)
6. _____ skate
7. Chick's noise
9. _____ the book
11. Isaiah, abbr.
17. ___, myself, and I

18. _____ my valentine

#13 PUZZLE

ACROSS

1. Egypt, abbr.
3. Small amount, also a letter of the Greek alphabet
7. "The Lord God. . .breathed into his nostrils the ____ ____ life; and man became a living soul" (2 words) (Gen. 2:7)
9. Benjamin's nickname
10. A name for Mother
11. What you say when you see a mouse
12. Arkansas, abbr.
13. Licensed nurse, abbr.
14. Telephone company
16. Stomach muscles, for short
17. Charged particle
19. A religious know-it-all in Christ's day
23. A biblical city in Syria on the coast near Sidon
24. Street, abbr.

DOWN

1. Grow less
2. "I have seen the wicked in great power, and spreading himself like a ____ ____ tree" (2 words) (Ps. 37:35)

3. Pronoun for a thing
4. Exclamation
5. These fruits are often thought of as vegetables
6. Not close
8. Compass point
13. Opposite of first

15. Muscle twitch
18. What Peter used for catching fish
20. Abbreviation for a physician
21. Delaware, abbr.

#14

ACROSS

1. Arkansas, abbr.
4. Guess
9. Negative
10. Undersea, treelike animal
11. Do, Old English
13. "Abraham. . .died. . .an _____ man" (Gen. 25:8)
14. Built by the sons of Elpaal (1 Chron. 8:12)
15. Not busy
16. Places where water is drawn from the ground
18. Emergency room, abbr.
19. "If any man that is called a brother be. . .an idolater, or a _____. . .with such an one no not to eat" (1 Cor. 5:11)
21. Edward's nickname

DOWN

1. Little word used to tell where something is
2. The kind of people Jesus said could get into heaven less easily than a camel could get through the eye of a needle (Matt. 19:24)
3. The well beside which Gideon camped (Judg. 7:1)

4. "He shall surely _____ her to be his wife" (Exod. 22:16)
5. The opposite of later
6. Medical officer, abbr.
7. The opposite of shorter
8. "Rebuke not an _____" (1 Tim. 5:1)
12. Place where the children of Judah settled (1 Chron. 4:29)
15. Small piece of land surrounded by water
17. Long Island, abbr.
20. Education, abbr.

PUZZLE #15

ACROSS

1. What comes before twos
5. Make a mistake
8. A word to describe the Spirit
9. A kind of snake
10. Infrared, abbr.
11. The opposite of down
12. Pay a call on someone
15. Yes in Spanish
16. Italian, abbr.
17. Bearing weapons
19. Purple Heart, abbr.
20. The little word that goes before a noun that begins with a vowel
21. Period of time
23. Tiny hole in your skin
26. What took Isaac's place when Abraham was going to sacrifice him
27. Fight

DOWN

1. Ohio, abbr.
2. The opposite of yes
3. Belonging to the man who took care of Samuel in the temple
4. Biblical country that bordered Israel
5. East bound, abbr.
6. "Judah is a lion's whelp:. . .who shall

_____ him up?"
(Gen. 49:9)
7. Fast
12. Snake
13. An Israelite
(2 Sam. 17:25)
14. Captures

18. I, J, K, L, __, __, __, __
22. Who God told
Abraham He was: I
_____ (Exod. 3:14)
24. Resident Assistant,
abbr.
25. Emergency room, abbr.

#16

ACROSS

1. Paddles
5. "Thou _____ them away as with a flood; they are as a sleep" (Ps. 90:5)
9. _____ upon a time
10. A kind of doctor's degree, abbr.
11. Chaplain, abbr.
12. When Abram pitched his tent, this city was to the east (Gen. 12:8)
13. Belonging to Shechem's father (Gen. 33:19)
15. Hurtful
16. Exclamation of triumph
18. A son of Benjamin (Gen. 46:21)
19. City built by Rehoboam (2 Chron. 11:5–6)
20. Certain

DOWN

1. Places where fruit trees grow
2. _____ you ready?
3. Rhode Island, abbr.
4. To divide something
5. Company, abbr.
6. Keeps a ship from drifting
7. The father of scribes (1 Kings 4:3)
8. Touch down, abbr.

12. "____, everyone that thirsteth" (Isa. 55:1)
14. ____, myself, and I
15. South America, abbr.
17. God told Moses His name was I ____ (Exod. 3:14)
19. Emergency room, abbr.

PUZZLE #17

ACROSS

1. A person's upper limbs
5. Our Savior
7. Body odor, abbr.
8. "_____, such a one! turn aside, sit down here" (Ruth 4:1)
10. "Do ye as _____ as ye drink" (1 Cor. 11:25)
12. A man in the Bible who lost everything
13. The opposite of on
14. "Ye tithe mint and _____" (Luke 11:42)
15. Nebraska, abbr.
16. Grand Duchess, abbr.
17. This man went to heaven in a fiery chariot
22. Healing plant

DOWN

1. Open up and say _____
2. Railroad, abbr.
3. Do, re, _____
4. Sunday school, abbr.
5. Hot drink
6. However
7. Favor or request
9. Son of Boaz (1 Chron. 2:12)

11. Task force, abbr.
12. Sr.'s son
18. Fa, so, _____
19. Illinois, abbr.
20. Josephine's nickname
21. Two vowels

#18 PUZZLE

ACROSS

1. "Uzzah and ___" (2 Sam. 6:3)
5. To make different
7. Company, abbr.
8. ___ what?
10. Opposite of in
12. Tin container
13. What's left after a fire
14. Greasy substance
15. Fa, so, la, ____
16. Set down
17. The opposite of days
21. "Make thy ____ thy footstool" (Acts 2:35)

DOWN

1. Open up and say ____
2. Laughter sound
3. Not out
4. "____, whom ye utterly destroyed" (Josh. 2:10)
5. Your uncle's child
6. Another way to spell Isaiah (Matt. 13:14)
7. Jacket
9. You can have ____ one
11. Thursday, abbr.

12. Young male horses
18. In full, abbr.
19. Leave
20. Not a she

#19

ACROSS

1. This man built a very large boat
5. "____, Patrobas" (Rom. 16:14)
7. "____, I come to do thy will" (Heb. 10:9)
8. Not a she
10. Editor, abbr.
11. Perfect
14. Gibeon was greater than this place (Josh. 10:2)
15. Shapes
16. Laugh noise
17. ___, myself, and I
18. "Children of ____" (Ezra 2:42)
23. What you say to a baby when they shouldn't do something

DOWN

1. Nebraska, abbr.
2. Operating room, abbr.
3. I ____
4. Not she
5. Naham's sister (1 Chron. 4:19)
6. An Israelite (1 Chron. 7:37)
7. Jacob's first wife (Gen. 29:23)
9. You better do this or ____

11. "_____ it be thou, bid me come" (Matt. 14:28)
12. Accomplish
13. Emergency room, abbr.
19. Small word that comes before a noun beginning with a vowel
20. Give that _____ me
21. Not out
22. Turn over, abbr.

#20 PUZZLE

ACROSS

1. Head coverings
5. Sixth book of the Bible
7. Alcoholics Anonymous, abbr.
8. Not she
9. Roman Catholic, abbr.
11. 200 in Roman numerals
12. Give it _____ me
13. Turn over, abbr.
14. Look, in King James English
16. A greeting
17. Southbound, abbr.
18. Not off
19. Prefix that means "not"
20. Someone in your family
23. "Unto us _____ _____ is given: and the government shall be upon his shoulder" (2 words) (Isa. 9:6)

DOWN

1. "_____, come forth" (Zech. 2:6)
2. Burnt material
3. Small word, like "a" and "an"
4. Sunday, abbr.
5. Belonging to the man that saw a ladder going up into heaven
6. Legendary king of England

7. 5th book of the New Testament
10. Round, metal object used for money
14. The opposite of a win
15. Fasten it ____ the wall
21. Iowa, abbr.
22. The letter that comes after "em"

#21

ACROSS

1. Too
5. Evidences
7. South America, abbr.
8. Hospital Apprentice, abbr.
10. Operating room, abbr.
11. Good ____ gold
13. Ohio, abbr.
14. ____ this for me
15. ____, myself, and I
16. ____ my valentine
17. Leah's son (Gen. 30:18)
20. "Behold, ____" (2 Sam. 15:32)
21. Ancestor of Jesus (Luke 3:25)

DOWN

1. Arkansas, abbr.
2. "____, I come unto thee in a thick cloud" (Exod. 19:9)
3. ____ what?
4. Belonging to
5. A chief of the people (Neh. 10:14)
6. "Children of ____" (Ezra 2:42)
7. "Son of ____" (Num. 13:10)
9. "Sons of ____" (1 Chron. 7:12)
11. "Which ____ was" (2 Sam. 17:25)
12. Biblical place with a great well (1 Sam. 19:22)

PUZZLE

18. Rises in the east
19. Son of Noah

#22

ACROSS

1. "Michmash, and ____" (Neh. 11:31)
5. "Be likeminded. . .being of one ____, of one mind" (Phil. 2:2)
7. "For they ____ evil against thee" (Ps. 21:11)
9. ___ you know what time it is?
10. Stand _____
11. What ____ you do?
13. Swallowed
14. Less than two
15. Made the earth
16. Angry feelings
19. "A bruised ____ shall he not break" (Isa. 42:3)

DOWN

1. To perform
2. Frozen water
3. Jonathan, for short
4. "Huppim, and ___" (Gen. 46:21)
5. To pour oil upon one
6. One who owes something
7. "Son of ___" (1 Kings 4:14)
8. What your hair is when it's not your natural color

12. Bambi was one
13. Grown older
17. ___, myself, and I
18. School class that
involves the most
physical exercise, abbr.

#23

ACROSS

1. The son of Zeruiah (2 Sam. 2:13)
5. "As a bride _____ herself with her jewels" (Isa. 61:10)
9. Sound of laughter
10. Not a she but a __
11. Eleazar's son (Matt. 1:15)
16. Style
17. "The cities of. . ._____" (Josh. 13:31)
18. Kansas, abbr.
20. "Thou _____ over all" (1 Chron. 29:12)
25. Nourishment

DOWN

1. JoAnn's nickname
2. Operating room, abbr.
3. Little word you'd say before "apple"
4. Exist
5. Sound of satisfaction
6. Harm
7. Expression of gratitude
8. Lays eggs
12. Airspeed, abbr.
13. Thursday, abbr.
14. Note of the musical scale

15. "_____, everyone that thirsteth" (Isa. 55:1)
16. What is that _____?
19. Street, abbr.
21. In full, abbr.
22. Leave

23. Opposite of yes
24. Edward's nickname

#24

ACROSS

1. Word you use to tell where something is
3. Not yes
5. Leading edge, abbr.
7. The day that follows today
9. Letter that comes after "el"
10. Opening in a fence
11. A child of Dishan (Gen. 36:28)
13. Violent group
14. Boy's name
16. Teacher's assistant, abbr.
18. Suitcases
20. Bureau of Narcotics, abbr.
21. Letter that follows "em"
22. Alaska, abbr.

DOWN

1. Took in food
2. Thomas, for short
3. Opposite of yes
4. Large musical instrument, often used in church
5. This man's wife turned into a pillar of salt
6. Female sheep
8. Made a bell sound

PUZZLE

1	2		3	4		5	6
7				8			
9				10			
		11	12				
		13					
14	15					16	17
18				19			
20			21			22	

11. Man that Samuel cut into pieces (1 Sam. 15:33)
12. Places where the deer and the buffalo roam
14. Become less
15. Vehicle for a large family
16. Hot drink
17. "Ye have not, because ye ____ not" (James 4:2)
19. ____ apple

#25

PUZZLE

ACROSS

1. Long, long ___
4. Michigan Institute of Technology, abbr.
7. A gate (2 Kings 11:6)
8. A son of Gad (Gen. 46:16)
9. "Which maketh ___, Orion, and Pleiades, and the chambers of the south" (Job 9:9)
12. "Lest he ___ thee to the judge" (Luke 12:58)
13. Kemuel's son (Gen. 22:21)
14. "___, and Zabad" (Ezra 10:27)
18. Not new
19. I stubbed my big ___
20. It is, contraction
21. "Mount ___" (Num. 20:25)

DOWN

1. "___ did that which was right in the eyes of the Lord" (1 Kings 15:11)
2. "Up to ___" (2 Kings 9:27)
3. Places where fruit trees grow
4. "Hand of ___" (Ezra 8:33)
5. A son of Caleb (1 Chron. 4:15)
6. "My Country ___ of Thee"
10. "Straightway the spirit ___ him" (Mark 9:20)

11. "And the sons of ___"
    (1 Chron. 7:17)
14. Write quickly
15. This man took care of
    Samuel in the temple
16. Also
17. Not his

#26

PUZZLE

ACROSS

1. We are the ____ of God
7. Tidy
8. Word you use to tell where something is
10. Tennessee, abbr.
11. The doctor says, "Say ____ "
12. The sea that Moses parted
14. Who ____ you?
15. Anger
16. Wall that keeps water from flowing
17. Not off
18. Jesus is called the Lamb ____ God
20. Prefix that means "two"
21. Shellfish
23. One of the men who were thrown into the fiery furnace (Dan. 3:23)

DOWN

1. What Pharaoh was driving when he chased the Children of Israel (Exod. 14:23)
2. Not out
3. God said to Pharaoh, "____ my people go" (Exod. 5:1)
4. Daniel's nickname
5. Route, abbr.
6. Book of the Bible that follows Ezra

9. Water bird
11. Person who speaks Arabic
13. Delaware, abbr.
14. Advertisement, for short
18. Not young
19. Not near
21. California, abbr.
22. Name for Mother

#27

ACROSS

1. "Extol him that rideth upon the heavens by his name ____, and rejoice before him" (Ps. 68:4)
4. In full, abbr.
6. King of Sodom (Gen. 14:2)
7. "Taanach nor. . .____" (Judg. 1:27)
9. Ohio, abbr.
10. Where you go to buy things
12. Look, in King James language (Exod. 19:9)
13. Pits in the ground
14. "____ your beasts, and go" (Gen. 45:17)
16. The son of Abdiel (1 Chron. 5:15)
17. Esau was the father of these people (Gen. 36:9)
18. One of the twelve tribes of Israel
19. Swallow food
20. Not a she
21. "Huppim, and ___" (Gen. 46:21)

DOWN

1. "Ahaz begat ___" (1 Chron. 8:36)
2. Arkansas, abbr.
3. "Sons of ___" (1 Chron. 11:34)
4. An idol worshiper

5. What's above your eyes and below your hair
6. "Flax was ___" (Exod. 9:31)
8. "___ the devil, and he will flee from you" (James 4:7)
11. Go ___ church
15. Finished

#28

ACROSS

1. To prepare food
5. The opposite of remember
7. Not well
8. "Pispah, and __"
   (1 Chron. 7:38)
10. Opposite of yes
11. Exist
13. Uruguay, abbr.
14. Turn over, abbr.
15. Emergency room, abbr.
16. South America, abbr.
17. "To him that _____ his conversation aright will I shew the salvation of God" (Ps. 50:23)
20. "So shall they be _____ pained at the report of Tyre" (Isa. 23:5)
21. Menaham's father (2 Kings 15:14)

DOWN

1. Colossians, abbr.
2. Operating room, abbr.
3. Biblical king (1 Kings 4:19)
4. "Shoa, and ___" (Ezek. 23:23)
5. Things that you walk on
6. Reliable
7. Divide _____ two pieces
9. "Ulla; _____" (1 Chron. 7:39)

11. Son of Zophah
    (1 Chron. 7:37)
12. Made a mistake
18. A faithful pet
19. Priest that Samuel
    stayed with in the
    temple (1 Sam. 2:11)

#29

ACROSS

1. What God fed the Children of Israel with in the desert
5. Bet
7. Ohio, abbr.
8. What you say when something hurts
9. Ourselves
10. Not good
12. Period of time
13. Type of tree
14. "Thou anointest my head with _____" (Ps. 23:5)
15. You, in King James English
16. Either
18. God told Moses His name was I _____ (Exod. 3:14)
19. Son of Ahitub (1 Sam. 14:3)
21. Girl who opened the door for Peter after the angel released him from prison (Acts 12:13)

DOWN

1. Pa's wife
2. Many years _____
3. Not old
4. Not rated, abbr.
5. Some say this was the animal that

	1	2	3	4		
	5					6
7			8			9
10		11			12	
13					14	
15			16	17		18
		19			20	
	21					

swallowed Jonah
6. What David wrote
7. Does what one is told
9. Bathsheba's husband (2 Sam. 11:3)
11. Decimeter, abbr.
12. Executive order, abbr.

16. Exclamation of triumph
17. Do away with
19. What you say when someone looks at your tonsils
20. Alcoholics Anonymous, abbr.

#30

ACROSS

1. What Jesus did on the cross
4. "Therefore sprang there even of one. . .so many as the stars of the ____" (Heb. 11:12)
7. What people eat with bagels
8. You wear this with a suit
9. Where we will see Christ when He returns (2 words) (Matt. 24:30)
11. Road, abbr.
12. I ____
14. "And kissed his feet, and anointed them with the ____" (Luke 7:38)
18. Scold and complain
19. Foot piggy
20. Compass point
21. Lays eggs

DOWN

1. 551, in Roman numerals
2. Charged particle
3. Trade
4. "Their heart ____ destruction" (Prov. 24:2)
5. A young goat
6. Not no

10. Either
13. Mountain, abbr.
14. There is only ____ God
15. Boy's name
16. Same as Noah (Matt. 24:37)
17. Number of lepers that Jesus healed (Luke 17:17)

#31

ACROSS

1. Saul's new name after he saw Christ
5. Women carry these
7. Still
8. Machine used for carding cotton
10. Operating room, abbr.
11. God told Moses to tell Pharaoh that I ____ had sent him (Exod. 3:14)
13. Opposite of yes
14. "Men of ____" (Jer. 48:31)
17. Priest who was with Samuel in the temple (1 Sam. 1:17)
18. Be in debt
19. Used for seasoning foods
22. Seth's son (Gen. 5:6)

DOWN

1. ____ the dishes on the table
2. Arkansas, abbr.
3. Ourselves
4. A limb used for walking
5. Dangers
6. "I will lay ____ upon you" (Ezek. 37:6)
7. Joins two work animals
9. Used to smell
11. Open up and say ____

12. ___, myself and I
15. Fruit that is no longer green
16. More than one roe
20. Not out
21. Company, abbr.

#32 PUZZLE

ACROSS

1. "For he loveth our nation, and he _____ built us a synagogue " (Luke 7:5)
5. The youngest son of Jerubbaal (Judg. 9:5)
7. Leave
8. Ohio, abbr.
10. Olive _____
12. American Meat Institute, abbr.
13. "Built ___" (1 Chron. 8:12)
14. Damp
15. Early morning moisture
16. Answer, abbr.
17. Where Jesus went to be alone (Matt. 14:13)
20. Was a passenger in a car

DOWN

1. "_____, everyone that thirsteth" (Isa. 55:1)
2. Word that helps tell where
3. Thursday, abbr.
4. Laugh sound
5. Became a member
6. Small piece of time
7. Not bad
9. Strikes

11. The opposite of higher
12. "Hypocrites! for ye are as graves which appear not, and the men that walk over them are not _____ of them" (Luke 11:44)
18. _____ what?
19. Edwin's nickname

#33

ACROSS

3. "From ____" (2 Kings 17:24)
7. "Of the ____" (Num. 26:20)
9. Mary and Joseph found no room in the ___
10. Tree juice
11. Not off
12. Fa, so, la, ____
13. Form of Noah (Matt. 24:37)
15. Are we there ___?
16. Twisted together
19. Seth's son (Gen. 5:6)

DOWN

1. It's my ____
2. Taps gently
3. Not able
4. Thursday, abbr.
5. A greeting
6. Warmed
7. "The Lord turned again the captivity of ____" (Ps. 126:1)
8. Saliva
14. Female sheep
15. Opposite of no
17. Not out
18. Opposite of yes

#34

ACROSS

1. Where Joseph and Mary found Jesus when he was a child (Luke 2:46)
5. Industrial Engineer, abbr.
7. Eve's husband
9. Male human
11. Globe
13. Large vase
14. Night bird
15. Month of the Jewish calendar (Ezra 6:15)
18. Pretty _____ a picture
19. Man who was strong so long as his hair was never cut

DOWN

2. In the center
3. Pod vegetable
4. This man's mother, Hannah, sent him to live in the temple
6. Scriptures
7. A prophetess who had been waiting to see Jesus (Luke 2:36)
8. Empty flatland in England
10. Arkansas, abbr.
12. Right worthy, abbr.
16. A wall that blocks a river's flow

17. What Jesus rode into Jerusalem

#35

PUZZLE

ACROSS

1. "Moses was. . .mighty in words and in ____" (Acts 7:22)
6. Large wasp
7. Not cold
8. "Straightway the spirit ____ him" (Luke 9:42)
10. "Down to ___" (Judg. 14:19)
12. Thursday, abbr.
13. Jr.'s dad
14. Opposite of yes
15. What you hear with
17. What hens lay
19. The children of Israel camped between this place and the sea (Exod. 14:2)
21. "Why make ye this ___" (Mark 5:39)
22. Next to

DOWN

1. Do, Old English
2. Emergency room, abbr.
3. Went in
4. Pass out cards
5. The opposite of weakly
6. "Jecamiah, ____" (1 Chron. 3:18)

7. Opposite of love
9. Seth's son (Gen. 5:6)
11. Kansas, abbr.
16. Do away with
18. "There was a battle at
    ___" (2 Sam. 21:18)
20. Leave

#36

ACROSS

1. "Harim, ____" (Neh. 12:15)
5. Not rough
7. Mi, fa, so, la, ____
8. Arkansas, abbr.
10. Isaiah, abbr.
11. An Israelite (2 Sam. 17:25)
14. ____, myself and I
15. Belonging to the man who took of each kind of animal into a big boat
16. Emergency room, abbr.
17. Exclamation of satisfaction
18. A prophet of Antioch (Acts 11:28)
23. What comes before twos

DOWN

1. I ____
2. Will you ____ this for me?
3. Opposite of yes
4. ____ what time are you going?
5. A man who gathered his chariots against the Israelites (Judg. 4:13)
6. Tikvah's father (2 Kings 22:14)
7. "In the ____ of harvest I will say to the reapers, Gather ye together first the tares" (Matt. 13:30)
9. Itchy spots

11. Not out
12. Can I go _____ the con-
    cert?
13. Hospital Apprentice,
    abbr.
19. Let's _____ home
20. Arrival notice, abbr.

21. I want to _____ like Jesus
22. United States, abbr.

#37

ACROSS

1. Isaiah, abbr.
3. Not close
6. Bani was one (2 Sam. 23:36)
8. Not off
9. Either
10. Pronoun for a thing
12. Josephine, for short
13. Leave
14. June, abbr.
16. "Tower of ___" (Neh. 3:1)
19. Belonging to the son of Serug (Gen. 11:22)
20. Thursday, abbr.
21. Placed

DOWN

1. Not wise
2. South America, abbr.
3. Type of evergreen
4. Look ___ that
5. "Thou ____ over all" (1 Chron. 29:12)
7. Did you ___ that?
8. Orange juice, for short
11. Go ____ bed
14. "Extol him that rideth upon the heavens by his name ____," (Ps. 68:4)

15. Seth's son (Gen. 5:6)
17. Nahum, abbr.
18. "Sir, come down ___
    my child die"
    (John 4:49)

#38

ACROSS
1. "Children of ___" (Ezra 2:52)
7. "Daughter of ___" (2 Kings 22:1)
8. Judah's son (Gen. 38:2,4)
9. Man's title of respect
11. The opposite of night
14. When Jesus was born there was no room in the ___
15. An untruth
16. "Take thine ___, eat, drink" (Luke 12:19)
19. City built by the children of Gad (Num. 32:34–35)
21. Child of Shobal (Gen. 36:23)

DOWN
1. Sound you make when you laugh
2. "He hath clothed me with the garments of salvation...as a bride ___ herself with her jewels" (Isa. 61:10)
3. Participated in a race
4. "Children of ___" (Neh. 7:47)
5. "He that ___ a matter wisely shall find good" (Prov. 16:20)
6. Open up and say ___
9. Spanish yes

10. Not out
12. Defeated the Israelites
    (Josh. 7:4–5)
13. "____ are all the
    children of light"
    (1 Thess. 5:5)
17. ___ you going?
18. "When he had dipped
    the ____, he gave it to
    Judas" (John 13:26)
19. Sweet ____ sugar
20. "____ everyone that
    thirsteth" (Isa. 55:1)

#39

ACROSS

1. "The wolf _____ them, and scattereth the sheep" (John 10:12)
7. Copied
8. Emergency room, abbr.
10. Arkansas, abbr.
11. Easy, for short
12. The devil is the "prince of the power of the _____" (Eph. 2:2)
14. Another way to spell May
15. Small child
16. What Noah built
17. Pronoun for a thing
18. Thursday, abbr.
20. Spanish yes
21. Was in debt
23. Jesus came from this town

DOWN

1. Genesis tells the story of _____
2. Teacher's assistant, abbr.
3. Certified Public Accountant, abbr.
4. Not him
5. Edward's nickname
6. The king that was the son of Ahaz (2 Kings 16:20)
9. Uprising

1		2	3	4	5		6
	■	7				■	
8	9	■	10		■	11	
12		13	■	■	14		
15		■	■	■	16		
17		■	18	19	■	20	
■	■	21			22	■	
23							

11. "He that hath _____ to hear, let him hear" (Matt. 11:15)
13. Route, abbr.
14. A name for Mother
18. Trans World Airline, abbr.

19. Not him
21. The make-believe land where Dorothy went
22. Delaware, abbr.

#40 PUZZLE

ACROSS

1. "Broken, or ___" (Lev. 22:22)
7. Abused
9. Not out
10. Note on the musical scale
11. Not cooked
13. Tree juice
14. Not a he
15. The upper joint of your leg
16. Laughter sound
17. Single
18. "Whereto we have already ___" (Phil. 3:16)
22. Made a noise like an owl

DOWN

1. "Alvan, and ___" (Gen. 36:23)
2. ___ the Cross
3. Pronoun for a thing
4. ___, myself , and I
5. Emergency room, abbr.
6. Made late
7. King of Gomorrah (Gen. 14:2)
8. I like my ice cream cone ___ in chocolate
12. Us
13. Cast a light

19. Can you come ___ my house?
20. Account of, abbr.
21. Italian, abbr.

#41

PUZZLE

ACROSS

1. Not different
5. Gifts
9. Jacob's first wife (Gen. 29:25)
10. Exclamation of triumph
11. Perform
12. Half of the people of Israel followed this man (1 Kings 16:21)
13. Leave
14. Thursday, abbr.
15. Not off
16. "The scribes and the Pharisees began to _____ him vehemently" (Luke 11:53)
18. Small insect
19. Esau was the forefather of these people (Gen. 36:9)
21. Boy's name

DOWN

1. Where you sit
2. Remains of anything burnt
3. _____, myself and I
4. Biblical village (Josh. 15:34)
5. The _____ of frogs, one of the bad things that happened to the Egyptians
6. Write down

7. The king sat upon his
   ____
8. "The ____ salute you"
   (Phil. 4:22)
12. Ohio, abbr.
14. Son of Ishmael
    (Gen. 25:15)

17. Created the earth
18. Swallowed food
20. Illinois, abbr.

#42

PUZZLE

ACROSS

3. "Refine them as ____ is refined" (Zech. 13:9)
7. Belonging to me
8. 2, in Roman numerals
9. Not off
11. Arkansas, abbr.
12. Vice-consul, abbr.
13. Myself
14. Rhode Island
15. Extraterrestrial, for short
16. Stomach muscle, for short
17. Young adult, abbr.
18. Give it ____ me
19. Not yes
20. Group of singers

DOWN

1. Hello, for short
2. A name for myself
3. Where the Chaldeans spoke to the king (Dan. 2:4)
4. We are to be dead to sin, but ____ ____ God (2 words) (Rom. 6:10)
5. The person who wins
6. 6th book of the New Testament
7. The mother of Jesus

10. Mountain where
    Moses died
    (Deut. 32:49–50)
21. "_____ everyone that
    thirsteth" (Isa. 55:1)
22. Ourselves

#43

PUZZLE

ACROSS

1. Married Jezebel
   (1 Kings 16:30–31)
4. Nebraska, abbr.
6. Children of Israel were
   defeated by the people of
   this city (Josh. 7:4)
7. Thursday, abbr.
9. Samuel served with this man in the
   temple
11. A son of Jether (1 Chron. 7:38)
12. Do away with
13. Anything that puts ourselves ahead
    of God
14. Isaiah, abbr.
15. Something to write with
16. What you say when someone
    looks at your tonsils
17. A shorter abbreviation for Isaiah
19. South America, abbr.
20. "The partridge sitteth on eggs, and
    ____ them not" (Jer. 17:11)
23. "Take ye ____" (Mark 13:33)

DOWN

2. Laughter sound
3. Two vowels
4. Baruch's father (Jer. 32:12)

5. Elijah's friend
   (2 Kings 2:1)
7. "O Lord. . .that _____
   the reins" (Jer. 11:20)
8. Mother of Samuel
   (1 Sam. 1)
17. Frozen water
18. Not a he
21. Thursday, abbr.
22. Editor, abbr.

#44

ACROSS

2. Food in a bowl
6. Jewish woman who became the queen of Persia
8. Be sick
9. The fourth Gospel, abbr.
10. Latin word that means "therefore"
12. Edward's nickname
13. Exist
14. Moabite woman who was the ancestor of David and Christ
16. Prefix that means "used to be"
17. 1st month of the year, abbr.
18. The sister of Mary and Lazarus
19. Theodore, for short

DOWN

1. An evil Old Testament woman (1 Kings 18:13)
2. Male deer
3. State in the east central U.S.
4. A son of Bani (Ezra 10:34)
5. Puerto Rico, abbr.
7. "Come _____ _____, all ye that fear God" (2 words) (Ps. 66:16)
9. Airplane
11. Name for a dog

14. Not common
15. "_____ us a son is given" (Isa. 9:6)
17. A name for God (Ps. 68:4)
18. Mountain, abbr.

#45

ACROSS

1. Years the Israelites spent in the wilderness, Jesus spent the same number of days there
6. You learn _____ school
8. Mindful
9. "Reel _____ and fro " (Isa. 24:20)
10. Part of the handwriting on the wall (Daniel 5:25)
11. 21st letter of the Greek alphabet
12. An altar (Josh. 22:34)
13. The biggest continent
15. A son of Haman (Est. 9:8–10)
17. Opposite of lose
19. Zuph's son (1 Chron. 6:34–35)
20. Another son of Haman (Est. 9:8–10)
22. Another name for Peter (Luke 6:14)

DOWN

1. When everyone knows who you are
2. Was in debt
3. "And _____ greedily after the error" (Jude 11)
4. Step
5. "_____ are spies" (Gen. 42:9)

6. A son of Uzziah
   (Neh. 11:4)
7. King of Hamath
   (2 Sam. 8:9)
11. Flies a plane
14. Lucifer
15. "Eshtemoh, and _____"
    (Josh. 15:50)
16. "_____, she is broken"
    (Ezek. 26:2)
17. "Before Abraham ___, I
    am" (John 8:58)
18. A son of Bela
    (1 Chron. 7:7)
21. Perform

#46

PUZZLE

ACROSS

1. Abraham's firstborn (Gen. 16:11)
8. "Bethbirei, and at ____." (1 Chron. 4:31)
10. One who inherits
11. The air above us
12. Not out
13. Type of hawk (Lev. 11:14)
15. "Declare good to the king with one ____" (2 Chron. 18:12)
17. Do away with
19. Boat team
20. "From _____ even" (Esther 1:1)
22. Perform
23. Father of King Saul (1 Sam. 9:3)

DOWN

1. Zoheth's father (1 Chron. 4:20)
2. "Set it between Mizpeh and ____" (1 Sam. 7:12)
3. "Between Bethel and ____;" (Gen. 13:3)
4. Belonging to the author of the second Gospel
5. Arkansas, abbr.
6. Resurrection day
7. "Who. . .can be ____ unto the Lord?" (Ps. 89:6)

9. Belonging to me
14. Milcah's brother (Gen. 11:29)
15. Melchi's father (Luke 3:28)
16. "_____ wings of a great eagle," (Rev. 12:14)
17. Rhode Island, abbr.
18. Colored writing fluid
21. Island, abbr.

#47

ACROSS

1. Exist
3. A family of the children of Asher (Num. 26:44)
8. The clock strikes 12 _____ midnight
9. Hunter constellation
10. Son of Abdiel (1 Chron. 5:15)
12. Son of Aram (Gen. 10:23)
13. "In _____ was there a voice" (Matt. 2:18)
15. I _____, God's name for Himself
17. Son of Helem (1 Chron. 7:35)
18. "And _____ greedily after the error" (Jude 11)
20. King Ahaziah was wounded by Jehu's men on the way to here (2 Kings 9:27)
22. Perform
23. "_____, on the north side" (Josh. 15:10)
26. "_____, and Bethpalet," (Josh. 15:27)

DOWN

1. Wife of Shaharaim (1 Chron. 8:8)
2. The encampment after Succoth (Num. 33:6)
3. JoAnn's nickname
4. Caleb's son (1 Chron. 4:15)
5. "The hill _____" (Ps. 42:6)

6. Not yes
7. ____ apple
11. Pictures
14. Encampment in the wilderness (Num. 33:13)
16. "He sent to Jobab king of ______" (Josh. 11:1)
19. Elishama's son (1 Chron. 7:26–27)
21. Male goat, Isaac's replacement on the altar
23. Church, abbr.
24. Not she
25. "For, ___, the winter is past," (Song of Sol. 2:11)

#48

PUZZLE

ACROSS

1. Hebrews, abbr.
4. 1st month of the Hebrew calendar (Exod. 13:4)
8. Mistake
9. Keeper of the women in Esther's time (Esther 2:3)
10. Isaiah, abbr.
12. Not yes
13. "Syrians of _____" (2 Sam. 10:8)
15. Jesus is the ____ of God
16. Frozen water
17. Bottom edge of a garment
18. "Either good ___ bad" (Gen. 31:24)
19. An Ishmaelite camel driver (1 Chron. 27:30)
21. "Azariah, Raamiah, _____" (Neh. 7:7)
24. Trap
25. "___ are spies" (Gen. 42:9)

DOWN

1. Not she
2. Judah's firstborn (Gen. 38:2–3)
3. "They take a _____, and they turn aside the poor" (Amos 5:12)
4. Open your mouth and say ____
5. Exist

6. "Then cometh also contempt, and with _____ reproach" (Prov. 18:3)
7. "Nebo, and _____" (Num. 32:3)
11. South America, abbr.
13. "For _____ sake" (Isa. 62:1)
14. Pagiel's father (Num. 1:13)
15. A son of Cush (Gen. 10:7)
17. Where you live
20. Untruth
22. Laughter noise
23. Arkansas, abbr.

#49

ACROSS

1. Son of Abdiel
(1 Chron. 5:15)
4. Irijah, a captain of the
____ (Jer. 37:14)
8. Hosea, abbr.
9. An ally of Abraham's (Gen. 14:13)
10. "To meet the Lord in the _____:"
(1 Thess. 4:17)
12. "Reel ___ and fro " (Isa. 24:20)
13. Belonging to the father of Josaphat
(Matt. 1:8)
15. Tree juice
16. Micah, abbr.
17. A son of Benjamin (Gen. 46:21)
18. Myself
19. Lease
21. "Terror. . .and the burning ____"
(Lev. 26:16)
24. Opposite of old
25. A group of cows
26. Perform

DOWN

1. "___ Lord God! behold" (Jer. 1:6)
2. "____, everyone that thirsteth"
(Isa. 55:1)
3. Abraham's son
4. Fight between countries
5. Small word that goes before a noun
beginning with a vowel

1	2	3	■	4	5	6	7
8			■	9			
■	■	10	11		■	12	
13	14			■	15		
16			■	17			■
18			■	19			20
21		22	23	■	24		
25				■	■	26	

6. "I _____ no strength"
   (Dan. 10:8)
7. Let fall
11. Island, abbr.
13. A hill near Gibeon
    (2 Sam. 2:24)
14. "Lay _____ against it, and
    build a fort" (Ezek. 4:2)
15. "Set it between Mizpeh
    and _____"
    (1 Sam. 7:12)
17. Judah's firstborn
    (Gen. 38:2–3)
20. "_____ wings of a great
    eagle" (Rev. 12:14)
22. Abraham's birthplace
    (Gen. 11:28)
23. An altar (Josh. 22:34)

#50

ACROSS

1. "Saul the son of _____," (Acts 13:21)
4. Opposite of went
8. "Lord, how _____ shall my brother sin against me, and I forgive him?" (Matt. 18:21)
9. Makes use of
10. Staff
12. Exist
13. Cliff
15. United Kingdom, abbr.
16. Legal rules
17. Jesus, the _____ of God
19. God said, "I _____"
20. A prophetess in the Gospel of Luke
22. Make clean
25. What you use to hear
26. Tribal enemy of Israel (Ezek. 23:23)
27. "_____ is God's throne" (Matt. 5:34)

DOWN

1. Company, symbol
2. You can have dessert, _____ you eat your vegetables
3. "The lion shall eat _____ like the ox" (Isa. 11:7)
4. Cows chew this
5. Black _____ coal

Across

Down

6. One of David's mighty men (2 Sam. 23:27)
7. Isaac's well of strife (Gen. 26:20)
11. The king of Bashan (Num. 21:33)
13. Talons
14. A city in Benjamin (Josh. 18:25)
17. South America, abbr.
18. We believe in _____ God
21. Paintings, sculptures, etc.
23. _____ what?
24. Laughter sound

#51

ACROSS

1. "___ Lord God! behold," (Jer. 1:6)
3. "Go and sell that thou ___" (Matt. 19:21)
7. Ikkesh was one (2 Sam. 23:26)
9. "To meet the Lord in the ___" (1 Thes. 4:17)
10. ___ apple
11. Wool gets spun into this
13. "The latter ___" (Ruth 3:10)
14. Elderly
15. Opposite of subtract
16. Opposite of down
17. Encounter
18. "___ shall see God." (Matt. 5:8)
21. Route, abbr.
22. Rabbit
23. Not she

DOWN

1. You learn ___ school
2. Listened
3. The mountain that was Aaron's grave (Deut. 32:50)
4. The city where Joshua had his first defeat (Josh. 7:4)
5. "The foundation of God ___" (2 Tim. 2:19)

The crossword grid with numbered cells: 1, 2, 3, 4, 5, 6 (top row); 7, 8 (second row); 9, 10 (third row); 11, 12, 13 (fourth row); 14, 15 (fifth row); 16, 17 (sixth row); 18, 19, 20, 21 (seventh row); 22, 23 (eighth row).

6. "The thoughts of the diligent _____ only to plenteousness" (Prov. 21:5)
8. Relatives
11. Opposite of old age
12. Jesus is the _____ and the Omega (Rev. 1:8)
13. A son of Mushi (1 Chron. 23:23)
15. A name for God, I _____
19. Emergency room, abbr.
20. "_____ are spies;" (Gen. 42:9)

#52

ACROSS

1. _____ what?
3. "Pitched at _____." (Num. 33:27)
8. Arkansas, abbr.
9. "_____, and Idbash:" (1 Chron. 4:3)
10. Untruth
12. Not she
13. Underground rodent
15. South America, abbr.
17. A prophetess in the Gospel of Luke
18. Attached to the hand
20. In the past
22. Sweaty class, abbr.
23. American Library Association, abbr.
24. _____ apple
25. The Philistine kings made gold ones to appease the Lord (1 Sam. 6:4)

DOWN

1. Boaz's father (1 Chron. 2:11)
2. Hunter constellation
3. Fa, so, la, _____, do
4. What's left after a fire
5. Son of Zorobabel (Luke 3:27)
6. I _____ leaving now

7. Laugh noise
11. "The sons of _____,"
    (1 Chron. 11:46)
14. Winged symbol of
    America
16. "_____: for they have
    heard evil tidings"

(Jer. 49:23)
19. Belonging to male
    adults
21. Boat paddle

#53

ACROSS

1. The king of Bashan (Num. 21:33)
3. Onam's son (1 Chron. 2:28)
7. What Hosea said to say to your sisters (Hos. 2:1)
9. The encampment before Dibongad (Num. 33:45)
10. Exist
11. Opposite of hot
13. Jeremiah, abbr.
14. "How long. . .____ thou be quiet?" (Jer. 47:6)
15. The mountain that was Aaron's grave (Deut. 32:50)
16. ____ apple
17. A Canaanite city (Josh. 11:21)
19. Heber's father (Luke 3:35)
22. Swallowed food
23. Seth's son (Gen. 4:26)
24. Not she

DOWN

1. "Either good ____ bad." (Gen. 31:24)
2. "Keep thy tongue from evil, and thy lips from speaking ___" (Ps. 34:13)
3. Like jelly
4. I ____
5. Place that bordered the land of the children of Zebulon (Josh. 19:12)

6. The father of the Hushim (1 Chron. 7:12)
8. Concealed
11. "Day and night shall not ____" (Gen. 8:22)
12. "The threshingfloor of _____" (1 Chron. 21:15)
13. Cephas's father (John 1:42)
15. Laughter sound
18. Buzzing stinger
20. "For, ___, the winter is past," (Song of Sol. 2:11)
21. Pretty ____ a picture

#54

ACROSS

1. International Harvester, abbr.
3. Measles symptom
7. What Jesus said to the girl who had died (Mark 5:41)
9. A city of the priests (1 Sam. 22:11)
10. Sly _____ a fox
11. Told an untruth
13. Flying mammal
14. It is, contraction
15. Girl, slang
16. Ohio, abbr.
17. Father of Anak (Josh. 21:11)
19. Amos' father (Luke 3:25)
22. "Of Keros, the children of _____," (Neh. 7:47)
23. How big something is
24. Mom

DOWN

1. "___ is God's throne." (Matt. 5:34)
2. "Came to _____." (Isa. 30:4)
3. Eve was made from Adam's
4. Sit _____ the table
5. Where the Amorites would dwell (Judg. 1:35)

6. "Go and sell that thou ____" (Matt. 19:21)
8. "____, Hadid, and Ono," (Ezra 2:33)
11. Kings of the jungle
12. One of David's mighty men (1 Chron. 11:31)
13. Part of a cage
15. Georgia, abbr.
18. American Automobile Association, abbr.
20. Son of Aram (Gen. 10:23)
21. Myself

#55

PUZZLE

ACROSS

1. Opposite of lose
4. Anub's father (1 Chron. 4:8)
7. ."The nobleman saith unto him, Sir, come down _____ my child die" (John 4:49)
8. Rehoboam's son (1 Chron. 3:10)
10. Belonging to Jacob's daughter (Gen. 30:21)
12. "_____ the Ahohite," (1 Chron. 11:29)
14. Alaska, abbr.
15. A prince of Babylon (Jer. 39:3)
18. A family of returned exiles (Ezra 2:57)
19. What happens to iron when it's exposed to water and air
22. Jerahmeel's wife (1 Chron. 2:26)
24. Concealed
25. Physical education, abbr.

DOWN

1. "Forgive us our debts as, ___ forgive our debtors" (Matt. 6:12)
2. Infrared, abbr.
3. A son of Jeconiah (1 Chron. 3:18)
4. Able
5. Obadiah, abbr.
6. "_____ and Gispa" (Neh. 11:21)
9. Question
11. The encampment before Dibongad (Num. 33:45)

1	2	3	■	4	5	6	■
7			■	8			9
■		10	11				
12	13			■		14	
15			■	16	17	■	
18			■	19		20	21
■	22	23					
■	24			■	25		

12. "And _____ also the Jairite" (2 Sam. 20:26)
13. Lamentations, abbr.
16. "The wilderness of Judah, which lieth in the south of _____;" (Judg. 1:16)
17. King Ahaziah was wounded by Jehu's men on the way to here (2 Kings 9:27)
20. Tree juice
21. "God created _____ heaven" (Gen. 1:1)
23. Note on the musical scale

#56

ACROSS
1. Single
4. Grow less
7. Decay
8. Jesus is called the _____ of David (Rev. 5:5)
10. Mistakes
12. Parcel of land
14. Extended play, abbr.
15. "Taste not, _____ not" (Col. 2:21)
18. Hezekiah's mother (2 Kings 18:2)
19. The book of the Bible that follows 2 Chronicles
24. Opposite of no
25. Near

DOWN
1. "Either good _____ bad" (Gen. 31:24)
2. Negative
3. How long heaven will last
4. Make a mistake
5. What a ghost says
6. Fail to interest
9. Teaspoon, abbr.
11. Color of blood
12. Expression of surprise
13. Taxi
16. Belonging to Lee

PUZZLE

1	2	3		4	5	6	
7				8			9
		10	11				
12	13					14	
15				16	17		
18				19		20	21
			23				
		24				25	

17. Ezra, abbr.
20. Eve was made from Adam's
21. No matter which
23. Masculine pronoun

#57

ACROSS

1. Joshua, abbr.
4. Abia's son (Matt. 1:7)
7. "Do ye, as _____ as ye drink" (1 Cor. 11:25)
8. Not straight
10. Reply
12. Piece of a skeleton
14. Belonging to me
15. Peter's brother
18. "That at the _____ of Jesus every knee should bow" (Phil. 2:10)
21. One of Ashur's wives (1 Chron. 4:5)
23. Machine used to card cotton
24. Note on the musical scale

DOWN

1. Short for Josephine
2. "An apostle ___ Jesus Christ" (1 Tim. 1:1)
3. Not sitting
4. Abdominal muscles, for short
5. To stitch
6. A Levite city within the tribe of Issachar (1 Chron. 6:73)
9. To test
11. Saul's grandfather (1 Chron. 8:33)

12. Barbara's nickname
13. Not off
16. Father of Ahira
    (Num. 1:15)
17. Fight between
    countries
19. Small rug

20. A son of Benjamin
    (Gen. 46:21)
22. The city where Joshua
    had his first defeat
    (Josh. 7:4)

#58

ACROSS

1. Concealed
4. Ephesians, abbr.
7. A son of Bela (1 Chron. 7:7)
8. "Sow in tears shall _____ in joy" (Ps. 126:5)
10. People committed to God
12. Poisonous snakes (Job 20:16)
14. A son of Dan (Num. 26:42)
17. Allow
18. "God _____ power to help" (2 Chron. 25:8)
21. Elijah's apprentice
23. "Being _____ and grounded in love" (Eph. 3:17)

DOWN

1. Hello, for short
2. Infrared, abbr.
3. "Where is the _____ of this world? hath not God made foolish the wisdom of this world?" (1 Cor. 1:20)
4. "The Oznites: of _____" (Num. 26:16)
5. Writing tool
6. Head covers
9. Psalms, abbr.
11. What's left after a fire
12. American sign language, abbr.

PUZZLE

13. Opposite of he
15. Gedor's brother
    (1 Chron. 8:31)
16. Sails are fastened to
    this
19. "God created ___
    heaven" (Gen. 1:1)

20. "He said that he would
    destroy them, ____
    not Moses his chosen
    stood before him"
    (Ps. 106:23)
22. "For, ___, the winter is
    past" (Song of Sol. 2:11)

#59

PUZZLE

ACROSS

1. One of Job's friends (Job 32:2)
6. Physical education, abbr.
8. Abiel's father (1 Sam. 9:1)
9. Arkansas, abbr.
10. Wicked
11. Single
12. Belonging to me
13. Small pointed object
15. Slumbering
17. Jesus was born in a stable, because there was no room in the _____
19. Picnic pests
20. High-voiced male singer
22. Groups of flying insects

DOWN

1. "_____, and at Tolad" (1 Chron. 4:29)
2. "Solomon raised a _____(1 Kings 5:13)
3. A son of Bela (1 Chron. 7:7)
4. Grasps
5. Abraham's birthplace (Gen. 11:28)
6. "As the hart _____ after the water brooks" (Ps. 42:1)
7. "How long will it be _____ ye make an end of words?" (Job 18:2)
11. Jerahmeel's son (1 Chron. 2:25)

14. "____ against the fenced cities" (Zeph. 1:16)
15. A prophetess in the Gospel of Luke
16. Psalms, abbr.
17. It is, contraction
18. Opposite of old
21. "Either good ____ bad." (Gen. 31:24)

#60

ACROSS

1. Our planet
6. Myself
8. Enan's son (Num. 7:83)
9. Judah's firstborn (Gen. 38:2–3)
10. "Cast the net on the right ____" (John 21:6)
11. 21st letter of the Greek alphabet
12. "Reel ____ and fro " (Isa. 24:20)
13. Jacob's brother
15. An idol of Hamath (2 Kings 17:30)
17. Swallow food
19. A city of Judah (Josh. 15:34)
20. "____ our sister" (Rom. 16:1)
22. Negative
23. A son of Caleb (1 Chron. 2:50–51)

DOWN

1. Direction the wise men came from
2. Gedor's brother (1 Chron. 8:31)
3. "____ me, and deliver me out of great waters" (Ps. 144:7)
4. Many of these make a forest
5. Laugh sound
6. A servant of Esther's husband (Esther 1:10)
7. "The Oznites: of ____" (Num. 26:16)

11. Hurt
14. Rams, lambs and ewes
15. "The children of _____
    of Hezekiah"
    (Ezra 2:16)
16. One of the prophets in
    the Old Testament

17. Ephesians, abbr.
18. "Against Jerusalem,
    ____" (Ezek. 26:2)
21. Exist

#61

ACROSS

1. "The _____ is not dead" (Matt. 9:24)
4. Possess
6. Isaiah, abbr.
7. Committed the first murder
8. Not out
10. A grain
12. The prophet of the Old Testament that follows Daniel
16. A short greeting
17. Becomes sick
18. Prefix that means "not"
19. Paintings, statues, etc.
20. Belonging to Kim
22. Helps

DOWN

1. Old Testament prophet that follows Jonah
2. Abia's son (Matt. 1:7)
3. This man was thrown into a den of lions
4. Central eastern state
5. Not yes
9. Belonging to the prophet that follows Micah
11. Can containers

13. Paddles
14. Positions oneself in a chair
15. Requests
19. Alcoholics Anonymous, abbr.
21. Pronoun for a thing

#62

PUZZLE

ACROSS

1. King Jehoash's mother (2 Kings 12:1)
7. "Strife, seditions, _____" (Gal. 5:20)
9. Son of Shobal (Gen. 36:23)
10. Opposite of stop
11. Walked at the head of the line
12. Marsh grass
14. An altar (Josh. 22:34)
15. Arkansas, abbr.
16. A son of Eber (Gen. 10:25)
19. "____, everyone that thirsteth" (Isa. 55:1)
21. Throw
22. Abraham's birthplace (Gen. 11:28)
23. Web-spinning creature

DOWN

1. Belonging to the father of James and John (Matt. 4:21)
2. Enoch's son (Gen. 4:18)
3. God of Babylon (Isa. 46:1)
4. Island, abbr.
5. The city where Joshua had his first defeat (Josh. 7:4)
6. Keeper of the women in Esther's time (Esther 2:3)

7. "Coast was from _____" (Josh. 19:33)
8. "And Jacob ___ pottage" (Gen. 25:29)
12. "The heathen _____" (Ps. 46:6)
13. Judah's firstborn (Gen. 38:2–3)
17. Child's favorite seat
18. A prince of Midian (Josh. 13:21)
19. Aaron and he held up Moses' arms (Exod. 17:12)
20. "Either good ___ bad." (Gen. 31:24)

#63

ACROSS

1. "Made Nibhaz and _____," (2 Kings 17:31)
7. "Hidden wisdom, which God _____ before the world" (1 Cor. 2:7)
9. Timber
10. Judah's firstborn (Gen. 38:2–3)
11. A name for God (Ps. 68:4)
12. Imitate
14. An altar (Josh. 22:34)
15. Abraham's birthplace (Gen. 11:28)
16. A tree with sweet-smelling wood
19. Laugh sound
21. A family group
22. Ohio, abbr.
23. Creature with 8 legs

DOWN

1. "_____ of grapes" (Amos 9:13)
2. One of the wives of Lamech (Gen. 4:19)
3. Male sheep
4. Note on the musical scale
5. _____ apple
6. "_____ yourselves from idols" (1 John 5:21)
7. Thing

8. Not wet
12. Healed
13. "Either good ___ bad." (Gen. 31:24)
17. To dunk
18. Hezekiah's mother (2 Kings 18:2)

19. The mountain that was Aaron's grave (Deut. 32:50)
20. "___, Lord God! behold" (Jer. 1:6)

#64

ACROSS

1. Johanan's father (Jer. 40:8)
7. Illegal wife of Herod (Matt. 14:3–4)
9. First man
10. "For, ___, the winter is past" (Song of Sol. 2:11)
11. Nehemiah, abbr.
12. "I have _____ still" (Job 3:13)
14. I ____ going home
15. Abraham's birthplace (Gen. 11:28)
16. Took notice of
19. You study the Bible ____ Sunday school
21. One of David's mighty men (1 Chron. 11:31)
22. ____ what?
23. "_____, and the brethren" (Rom. 16:14)

DOWN

1. "_____ unto Sihon" (Deut. 2:26)
2. Haniel's brother (1 Chron. 7:39)
3. Romans, abbr.
4. An altar (Josh. 22:34)
5. The city where Joshua had his first defeat (Josh. 7:4)
6. "Helkath, and _____" (Josh. 19:25)

7. Heman's son
   (1 Chron. 25:4)
8. Jesus was the ____ of
   God
12. Mizraim's son
   (Gen. 10:13)
13. Arkansas, abbr.

17. "God created ____
   heaven" (Gen. 1:1)
18. Used to hear
19. Animal that saw an
   angel (Num. 22:23)
20. "Reel ____ and fro "
   (Isa. 24:20)

#65

ACROSS

1. This man was persecuted with Paul (Acts 13:50)
7. Width x height
8. New York, abbr.
9. Not good
10. Quick _____ a wink
12. Year, abbr.
13. Paintings, sculptures, etc.
14. Where a child likes to sit
15. Where food is grown
16. Old Testament, abbr.
17. Not near
18. "I _____ the pride of Judah" (Jer. 13:9)
19. Land of the Chaldees (Gen. 15:7)
20. "Thou didst increase thy _____s" (Isa. 57:9)

DOWN

1. "By the rivers of _____ there we sat down" (Ps. 137:1)
2. Mountain where the ark came to rest (Gen. 8:4)
3. The sea the Israelites crossed
4. North America, abbr.
5. _____ apple
6. The kind of tree Zaccheus climbed

1	2	3	4			5	6
7						8	
9				10	11		
12			13				
14				15			
16			17				
		18				19	
	20						

10. What a dog says: ____-
    ____

11. What the wise men
    followed

17. "The night is ____
    spent" (Rom. 13:12)

18. Myself

19. Syllable you say when
    you can't think what
    to say

#66

ACROSS

1. A son of Joktan (Gen. 10:29)
6. South Africa, abbr.
8. "He ____ in the synagogue" (Acts 18:4)
10. Judah's firstborn (Gen. 38:2–3)
11. A son of Issachar (Gen. 46:13)
12. To grab with your teeth
15. A name for God: I ____
16. A cover
17. A son of Benjamin (Gen. 46:21)
18. "Reel ___ and fro " (Isa. 24:20)
19. Small word used before a noun beginning with a vowel
20. Opposite of in
22. Where Mary did not find Jesus after His death
25. Zoheth's father (1 Chron. 4:20)
26. "___ that ye refuse" (Heb. 12:25)

DOWN

1. "Brought the heads of _____" Judg. 7:25
2. "In the last days ___ times shall come" (2 Tim. 3:1)
3. Sound of laughter
4. Island, abbr.
5. Decay

1	2	3	4	5	■	6	7
8					9		
10		■	■	11			
12		13	14	■		15	
■	16				17		
18		■	■	19		■	■
20		21	■	22		23	24
25				■	26		

6. A pause or musical notation used in the Psalms
7. A walled city in Naphtali (Josh. 19:33)
9. Negative
13. Note on the musical scale
14. An altar (Josh. 22:34)
17. Seth's son (Gen. 5:6)
18. King of Hamath (2 Sam. 8:9)
19. I'll see you _____ church
21. Thursday, symbol
23. Myself
24. Exist

#67

PUZZLE

ACROSS

1. A musical instrument similar to a piano
6. Note on the musical scale
8. "Plain of _____." (Judg. 9:37)
10. Good ____ gold
11. A son of Issachar (Gen. 46:13)
12. "He _____ upon a cherub" (Ps. 18:10)
15. The king of Bashan (Num. 21:33)
16. "Thy ____ and thy staff they comfort me" (Ps. 23:4)
17. Single
18. The sun rises ____ daybreak
19. Not off
20. Acquire
22. "In _____ was there a voice" (Matt. 2:18)
25. "Wise men out of _____" (Obad. 1:8)
26. Saul's grandfather (1 Chron. 8:33)

DOWN

1. Son of Eliphaz (Gen. 36:11)
2. "The multitude ____ unto him" (Mark 2:13)
3. Opposite of stop
4. ____ apple
5. What Peter and Andrew used for fishing

Crossword grid with numbered cells: 1, 2, 3, 4, 5, 6, 7 (top row); 8, 9; 10, 11; 12, 13, 14, 15; 16, 17; 18, 19; 20, 21, 22, 23, 24; 25, 26.

6. A son of Shimon
   (1 Chron. 4:20)
7. Picture
9. Not yes
13. Perform
14. An altar (Josh. 22:34)
17. Judah's secondborn
   son (Gen. 38:4)
18. Period of time
19. "Either good ___ bad."
   (Gen. 31:24)
21. "Reel ___ and fro"
   (Isa. 24:20)
23. Myself
24. Arkansas, abbr.

#68

PUZZLE

ACROSS

1. A son of Benjamin (1 Chron. 8:1–2)
6. The city where Joshua had his first defeat (Josh. 7:4)
8. Early nights
10. Exist
11. Father of Shem (Gen. 5:32)
12. "Brought the heads of _____" (Judg. 7:25)
15. "Reel ___ and fro" (Isa. 24:20)
16. To test
17. Sleeping place
18. _____ what?
19. Infrared, abbr.
20. Word that begins a question
22. "Land from _____ to" (Isa. 16:1)
25. A son of Ram (1 Chron. 2:27)
26. "In all the region of ____" (1 Kings 4:11)

DOWN

1. The mountain that was Moses' grave (Deut. 32:48–50)
2. Caught up with
3. Pronoun for a boy
4. Small word that comes before a noun beginning with a vowel
5. Liquid measure
6. A gem on the third row of the priest's breastplate (Exod. 28:15,19)
7. "Hammoleketh bare _____" (1 Chron. 7:18)

9. Not yes
13. Judah's firstborn (Gen. 38:2–3)
14. Near
17. The manna ____ worms when the people left it over night (Exod. 16:20)
18. Opposite of he
19. Island, abbr.
21. "Forgive us our debts, as ____ forgive our debtors" (Matt. 6:12)
23. "For, ____, the winter is past" (Song of Sol. 2:11)
24. Arkansas, abbr.

#69

ACROSS

1. "The golden _____"
   (Isa. 13:12)
5. South Africa, abbr.
7. I get up ____ daybreak
8. Command
10. "___ are spies " (Gen. 42:9)
11. "Whither have ye made a _____ to
    day?" (1 Sam. 27:10)
12. Peleg's son (Gen. 11:18)
15. ____ what?
16. Finishes
17. Jesus is the ____ of Man
18. Note on the musical scale
19. Tin container
20. Swallowed food
22. Jerahmeel's son (1 Chron. 2:25)
24. A city in Lycia (Acts 27:5)
25. Fuss

DOWN

1. Jesus is the ____, the truth and the
   life
2. Forever
3. Opposite of stop
4. Mistake
5. Flavored
6. A son of Caleb (1 Chron. 2:18)

9. Perform
13. An altar (Josh. 22:34)
14. We
16. Village in Simeon,
    (1 Chron. 4:32)
17. Abraham's wife
    (1 Pet. 3:6)

19. Company, abbr.
21. Judah's firstborn
    (Gen. 38:2–3)
23. Negative

#70 PUZZLE

ACROSS

1. Relatives
4. "_____ is the Lord" (Exod. 5:2)
7. "Thou wilt cast all their sins _____ the depths of the sea" (Mic. 7:19)
8. "_____ can a man be born when he is old?" (John 3:4)
9. Note on the musical scale
10. Odor
12. Grand
14. "They _____ it up" (Mic. 7:3)
15. "All your adversaries shall not be able to _____ nor resist" (Luke 21:15)
18. Opposite of boys
19. Myself
20. "Day of _____ birth" (Eccles. 7:1)
21. Island, abbr.

DOWN

1. Type of fabric
2. "___ is God's throne" (Matt. 5:34)
3. Nose holes
4. "I will meet them as a bear that is bereaved of her _____" (Hos. 13:8)
5. Word that describes the Spirit
6. Night flier

7. It is, contraction
11. "Lest by any _____ I should run. . .in vain" (Gal. 2:2)
13. Mindful
15. Machine for carding cotton

16. A family of returned exiles (Ezra 2:57)
17. "_____ verily, their sound went into all the earth" (Rom. 10:18)
18. Opposite of stop

#71

PUZZLE

ACROSS

1. Connected to the foot
4. Ephesians, abbr.
7. Injure
8. Greek form of Noah (Matt. 24:37)
9. Island, abbr.
10. "Sia, the children of _____" (Neh. 7:47)
12. "Deliver thee into the hand of brutish men, and _____ to destroy" (Ezek. 21:31)
14. We need to get the beam out of our own eye before we worry about this in our brother's
15. "Thou takest up that thou _____ not down," (Luke 19:21)
18. Simeon at Antioch was called this (Acts. 13:1)
19. The city where Joshua had his first defeat (Josh. 7:4)
20. Azariah's father (2 Chron. 15:1)
21. Physical education, abbr.

DOWN

1. Job
2. "Either good ___ bad." (Gen. 31:24)
3. Hired

4. "Tarry ye in the city of Jerusalem, until ye be ____ with power from on high" (Luke 24:49)
5. Small body of water
6. Zephaniah's son (Zech. 6:14)
7. Belonging to him
11. The opposite of before
13. Picture
15. A cover
16. Tree juice
17. Bind
18. Negative

#72

PUZZLE

ACROSS

1. He is love
4. _____ what?
6. Wheel on a car
7. Possession of
9. Not off
10. Abraham's father, Greek form (Luke 3:34)
12. Belonging to the man who was also called Jacob
14. Employ
15. "We were Pharaoh's _____" (Deut. 6:21)
18. "Jonah was gone down into the _____ of the ship" (Jon. 1:5)
19. "___ are spies " (Gen. 42:9)
20. Joseph mourned for Jacob at this man's threshing floor (Gen. 50:10)
21. Judah's firstborn (Gen. 38:2–3)

DOWN

1. Machines for carding cotton
2. "Either good ___ bad" (Gen. 31:24)
3. "_____ before the Lord" (1 Sam. 21:7)
4. "Jacob came to _____" (Gen. 33:18)

5. Boat paddles
6. King of Hamath (2 Sam. 8:9)
8. South America, abbr.
11. Groups of cows
13. She opened the door for Peter after he escaped from prison (Acts 12:13)
15. A tiny amount
16. Needed for vision
17. Saul's grandfather (1 Chron. 8:33)
18. South Africa, abbr.

#73

ACROSS

1. Routes, abbr.
4. Writing tool
7. These provide sight
9. Single
10. Arkansas, abbr.
11. A son of Bela (1 Chron. 8:3–4)
13. Act
15. Opposite of there
16. June, abbr.
17. Lud's brother (Gen. 10:22)
20. Elmodam's son (Luke 3:28)
22. Myself
23. Warmth
24. "___ is God's throne." (Matt. 5:34)

DOWN

1. "They that sow in tears shall _____ in joy" (Ps. 126:5)
2. "Ye to do with me, O _____" (Joel 3:4)
3. Stock exchange, abbr.
4. The opposite of richer
5. A city of Judah (Josh. 15:34)
6. Nehemiah, abbr.
8. Free from danger
12. King of Gezer (Josh. 10:33)
14. Son of Zorobabel (Luke 3:27)

16. Joseph's nickname
18. A family of returned exiles (Ezra 2:57)
19. Encountered
20. Church, abbr.
21. The stars come out _____ night

#74

ACROSS

1. Tiny winged insect
5. Belonging to things you chew with
7. The second judge of Israel (Judg. 3:15)
8. "And forgive us our debts, as ___ forgive our debtors" (Matt. 6:12)
10. A fenced city (Josh. 19:35)
11. Cattle feed
12. "I will ____ evil beasts" (Lev. 26:6)
13. "Sir, come down ____ my child die" (John 4:49)
14. Infrared, abbr.
15. Weapons
16. "Break the _____" (Ezek. 23:34)
19. "Used curious ____" (Acts 19:19)

DOWN

1. This plant gave Jonah shade (Jon. 4:6)
2. East of Eden (Gen. 4:16)
3. You learn ___ school
4. Thursday, abbr.
5. Belonging to them
6. "No ____ of flies shall be there" (Exod. 8:22)
7. Chelub's son (1 Chron. 27:26)
9. These provide sight

11. Groups of cows
15. Paintings, sculptures, etc.
17. Laughter sound
18. Judah's firstborn (Gen. 38:2–3)

#75

ACROSS

1. "Slew Hamor...with the ____ of the sword" (Gen. 34:26)
5. A son of David (2 Sam. 5:14–16)
7. Wept
8. Thursday, abbr.
10. Jether's son (1 Chron. 7:38)
11. Swallowed food
12. Saph was slain here (2 Sam. 21:18)
13. Not near
14. Judah's firstborn (Gen. 38:2–3)
15. "She is empty, and ____" (Nah. 2:10)
16. ____ blessed Joseph and Mary (Luke 2:34)
19. "Mordecai the Jew was ____ unto king Ahasuerus" (Esther 10:3)

DOWN

1. David's oldest brother (1 Sam. 17:13)
2. What Jesus did on the cross
3. A son of Jacob (Gen. 30:10–11)
4. An altar (Josh. 22:34)
5. Mistakes
6. "It is high, I cannot ____ unto it" (Ps. 139:6)
7. Where an animal is kept at the zoo

PUZZLE

9. Group of cows
11. "Ran _____ thither" (Mark 6:33)
15. "Awake that shall _____ thee" (Hab. 2:7)
17. Not out
18. Myself

PUZZLE #1

PUZZLE #2

PUZZLE #3

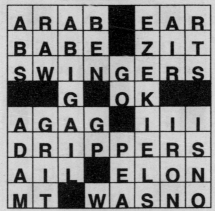

A	R	A	B			E	A	R
B	A	B	E		Z	I	T	
S	W	I	N	G	E	R	S	
			G		O	K		
A	G	A	G			I	I	I
D	R	I	P	P	E	R	S	
A	I	L			E	L	O	N
M	T		W	A	S	N	O	

PUZZLE #4

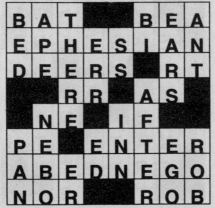

B	A	T			B	E	A	
E	P	H	E	S	I	A	N	
D	E	E	R	S		R	T	
		R	R		A	S		
	N	E		I	F			
P	E		E	N	T	E	R	
A	B	E	D	N	E	G	O	
N	O	R			R	O	B	

PUZZLE #5

PUZZLE #6

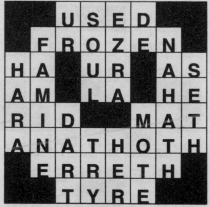

PUZZLE #7

PUZZLE #8

PUZZLE #9

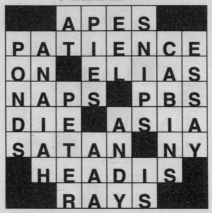

PUZZLE #10

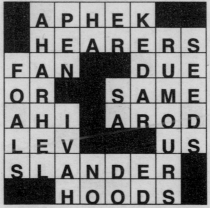

PUZZLE #11

PUZZLE #12

PUZZLE #13

PUZZLE #14

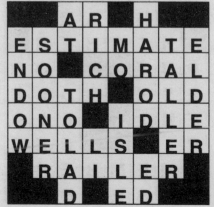

PUZZLE #15

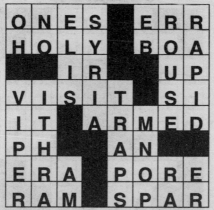

PUZZLE #16

PUZZLE #17

PUZZLE #18

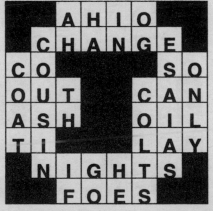

PUZZLE #19

	N	O	A	H	
	H	E	R	M	E	S
L	O				H	E
E	D		I	D	E	A	L
A	I		F	O	R	M	S
H	A				M	E
	H	A	T	I	T	A
	N	O	N	O	

PUZZLE #20

	H	A	T	S	
	J	O	S	H	U	A
A	A		H	E		R	C
C	C				T	O
T	O		L	O		H	I
S	B		O	N		U	N
	S	I	S	T	E	R
	A	S	O	N

PUZZLE #21

PUZZLE #22

PUZZLE #23

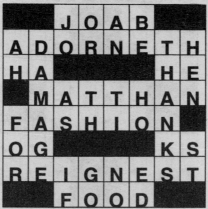

	J	O	A	B		
A	D	O	R	N	E	T	H
H	A				H	E
	M	A	T	T	H	A	N
F	A	S	H	I	O	N	
O	G				K	S
R	E	I	G	N	E	S	T
	F	O	O	D		

PUZZLE #24

A	T		N	O		L	E
T	O	M	O	R	R	O	W
E	M			G	A	T	E
			A	R	A	N	
			G	A	N	G	
E	V	A	N		T	A
B	A	G	G	A	G	E	S
B	N		E	N		A	K

PUZZLE #25

PUZZLE #26

PUZZLE #27

	J	A	H		I	F	
B	E	R	A		D	O	R
O	H		S	T	O	R	E
L	O		H	O	L	E	S
L	A	D	E		A	H	I
E	D	O	M	I	T	E	S
D	A	N			E	A	T
	H	E		A	R	D	

PUZZLE #28

	C	O	O	K			
	F	O	R	G	O	T	
I	L	L	-	A	R	A	N
N	O		B	E		U	R
T	O		E	R		S	A
O	R	D	E	R	E	T	H
	S	O	R	E	L	Y	
	G	A	D	I			

PUZZLE #29

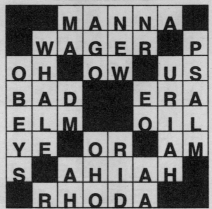

PUZZLE #30

PUZZLE #31

PUZZLE #32

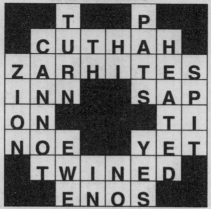

PUZZLE #35

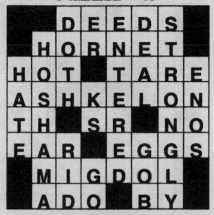

PUZZLE #36

PUZZLE #37

	I	S		F	A	R	
	G	A	D	I	T	E	
O	N		O	R		I	T
J	O				G	O	
R		J	E		N		
H	A	N	A	N	E	E	L
N	A	H	O	R	S		
T	H		S	E	T		

PUZZLE #38

H	A	R	S	H	A	
A	D	A	I	A	H	
O	N	A	N			
S	I	R		D	A	Y
I	N	N		L	I	E
	E	A	S	E		
A	T	R	O	T	H	
S	H	E	P	H	O	

PUZZLE #39

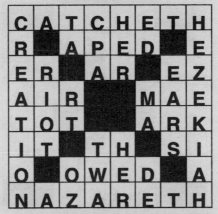

C	A	T	C	H	E	T	H	
R		A	P	E	D		E	
E	R		A	R		E	Z	
A	I	R			M	A	E	
T	O	T			A	R	K	
I	T		T	H		S	I	
O		O	W	E	D		A	
N	A	Z	A	R	E	T	H	

PUZZLE #40

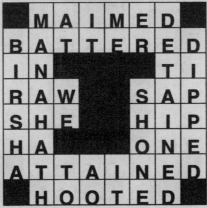

	M	A	I	M	E	D	
B	A	T	T	E	R	E	D
I	N				T	I	
R	A	W		S	A	P	
S	H	E		H	I	P	
H	A			O	N	E	
A	T	T	A	I	N	E	D
H	O	O	T	E	D		

PUZZLE #41

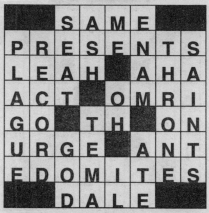

		S	A	M	E		
P	R	E	S	E	N	T	S
L	E	A	H		A	H	A
A	C	T		O	M	R	I
G	O		T	H		O	N
U	R	G	E		A	N	T
E	D	O	M	I	T	E	S
	D	A	L	E			

PUZZLE #42

		H		M			
	S	I	L	V	E	R	
M	Y	I	I	E	O	N	
A	R	V	C	M	E		
R	I	E	T	A	B		
Y	A	T	O	N	O		
	C	H	O	R	U	S	
	O			S			

PUZZLE #43

PUZZLE #44

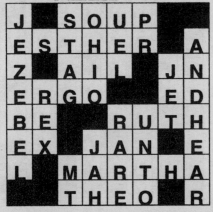

PUZZLE #45

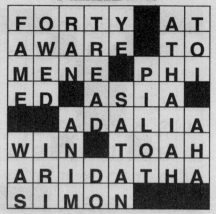

F	O	R	T	Y		A	T
A	W	A	R	E		T	O
M	E	N	E		P	H	I
E	D		A	S	I	A	
		A	D	A	L	I	A
W	I	N		T	O	A	H
A	R	I	D	A	T	H	A
S	I	M	O	N			

PUZZLE #46

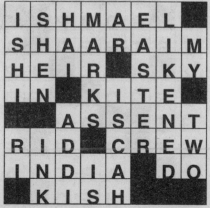

I	S	H	M	A	E	L	
S	H	A	A	R	A	I	M
H	E	I	R		S	K	Y
I	N		K	I	T	E	
		A	S	S	E	N	T
R	I	D		C	R	E	W
I	N	D	I	A		D	O
K	I	S	H				

PUZZLE #47

PUZZLE #48

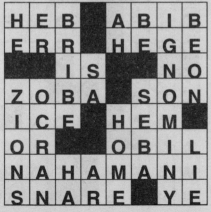

PUZZLE #49

PUZZLE #50

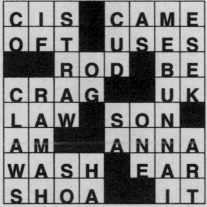

PUZZLE #51

PUZZLE #52

PUZZLE #53

PUZZLE #54

PUZZLE #55

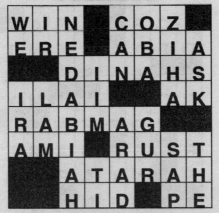

PUZZLE #56

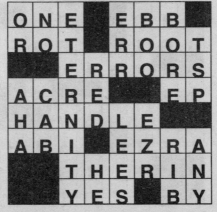

PUZZLE #57

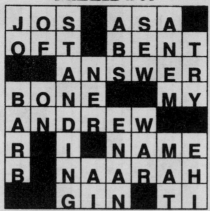

```
J O S   A S A
O F T   B E N T
      A N S W E R
B O N E     M Y
A N D R E W
R   I   N A M E
B   N A A R A H
    G I N   T I
```

PUZZLE #58

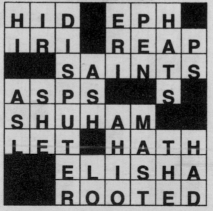

```
H I D   E P H
I R I   R E A P
    S A I N T S
A S P S     S
S H U H A M
L E T   H A T H
    E L I S H A
    R O O T E D
```

PUZZLE #59

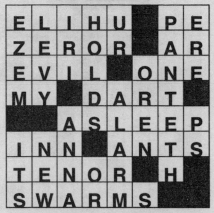

PUZZLE #60

PUZZLE #61

M	A	I	D		O	W	N
I	S		A		H		O
C	A	I	N		I	N	
A			I		O	A	T
H	O	S	E	A		H	I
	A	I	L	S		U	N
A	R	T		K	I	M	S
A	S	S	I	S	T	S	

PUZZLE #62

	Z	I	B	I	A	H	
H	E	R	E	S	I	E	S
E	B	A	L			G	O
L	E	D		R	E	E	D
E	D			A	R		
P	E	L	E	G		H	O
H	E	A	V	E		U	R
	S	P	I	D	E	R	

PUZZLE #63

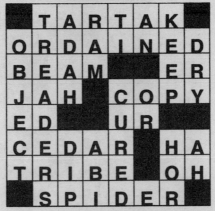

PUZZLE #64

PUZZLE #65

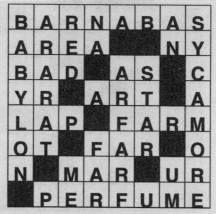

```
B A R N A B A S ·
A R E A · · · N Y
B A D · A S · C ·
Y R · A R T · A ·
L A P · F A R M ·
O T · · F A R · O
N · M A R · U R ·
· P E R F U M E ·
```

PUZZLE #66

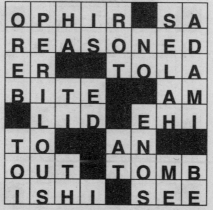

```
O P H I R · S A ·
R E A S O N E D ·
E R · · T O L A ·
B I T E · · A M ·
· · L I D · E H I
T O · A N · · · ·
O U T · T O M B ·
I S H I · S E E ·
```

PUZZLE #67

O	R	G	A	N	■	■	T	I	■
M	E	O	N	E	N	I	M	A	■
A	S	■	■	T	O	L	A	■	■
R	O	D	E	■	■	O	G	■	■
■	R	O	D	■	O	N	E	■	■
A	T	■	■	O	N	■	■	■	■
G	E	T	■	R	A	M	A	■	■
E	D	O	M	■	■	N	E	R	■

PUZZLE #68

N	O	H	A	H	■	■	A	I	■
E	V	E	N	I	N	G	S	■	■
B	E	■	■	N	O	A	H	■	■
O	R	E	B	■	■	T	O	■	■
■	■	T	R	Y	■	B	E	D	■
S	O	■	■	I	R	■	■	■	■
H	O	W	■	S	E	L	A	■	■
E	K	E	R	■	D	O	R	■	■

PUZZLE #69

PUZZLE #70

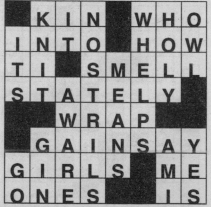

PUZZLE #71

PUZZLE #72

PUZZLE #73

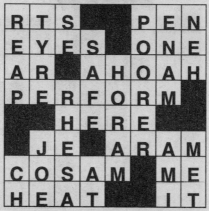

R	T	S			P	E	N
E	Y	E	S		O	N	E
A	R		A	H	O	A	H
P	E	R	F	O	R	M	
		H	E	R	E		
	J	E		A	R	A	M
C	O	S	A	M		M	E
H	E	A	T			I	T

PUZZLE #74

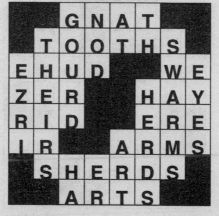

	G	N	A	T			
	T	O	O	T	H	S	
E	H	U	D			W	E
Z	E	R			H	A	Y
R	I	D			E	R	E
I	R			A	R	M	S
S	H	E	R	D	S		
	A	R	T	S			

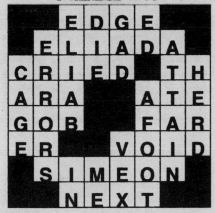

AWESOME BOOKS FOR KIDS!

The Young Reader's Christian Library
Action, Adventure, and Fun Reading!

This series for young readers ages 8 to 12 is action-packed, fast-paced, and Christ-centered! With exciting illustrations on every other page following the text, kids won't be able to put these books down! Over 100 illustrations per book. All books are paperbound. The unique size (4 ³⁄₁₆" x 5 ³⁄₈") makes these books easy to take anywhere!

A Great Selection to Satisfy All Kids!

Abraham Lincoln	*Heidi*	*Pollyanna*
Ben-Hur	*Hudson Taylor*	*Prudence of Plymouth*
Billy Graham	*In His Steps*	*Plantation*
Billy Sunday	*Jesus*	*Robinson Crusoe*
Christopher Columbus	*Joseph*	*Roger Williams*
Corrie ten Boom	*Lydia*	*Ruth*
David Brainerd	*Miriam*	*Samuel Morris*
David Livingstone	*Moses*	*The Swiss Family*
Deborah	*Paul*	*Robinson*
Elijah	*Peter*	*Taming the Land*
Esther	*The Pilgrim's Progress*	*Thunder in the Valley*
Florence Nightingale	*Pocahontas*	*Wagons West*

Available wherever books are sold.
Or order from: Barbour Publishing, Inc., P.O. Box 719
Uhrichsville, Ohio 44683
http://www.barbourbooks.com

$2.50 each retail, plus $1.00 for postage and handling per order. Prices subject to change without notice.